In the Year 1929

By

Kerry Butters.

In the Year 1929.

Millennium:	**2nd millennium**
Centuries:	19th century – **20th century** – 21st century
Decades:	1890s 1900s 1910s – **1920s** – 1930s 1940s 1950s
Years:	1926 1927 1928 – **1929** – 1930 1931 1932

1929 (MCMXXIX) was a common year starting on Tuesday (dominical letter F) of the Gregorian calendar, the 1929th year of the Common Era (CE) and *Anno Domini* (AD) designations, the 929th year of the 2nd millennium, the 29th year of the 20th century, and the 10th and last year of the 1920s decade. Note that the Julian day for 1929 is 13 days difference, and was the last year in which the Julian calendar continued to be used when complete conversion of the Gregorian calendar was entirely done.

This year marked the end of a period known in American history as the Roaring Twenties after the Wall Street Crash of 1929 ushered in a worldwide Great Depression. In the Americas, an agreement was brokered to end the Cristero War a Catholic counter-revolution in Mexico. The Judicial Committee of the Privy Council, a British high court, ruled that Canadian women are persons in the *Edwards v. Canada (Attorney General)* case. The 1st Academy Awards for film were held in Los Angeles, while the Museum of Modern Art opened in New York City. The Peruvian Air Force was created.

In Asia, the Republic of China and the Soviet Union engaged in a minor conflict after the Chinese seized full control of the Manchurian Chinese Eastern Railway, which ended with a resumption of joint administration. In the Soviet Union, General Secretary Joseph Stalin expelled Leon Trotsky and adopted a policy of collectivization. The Grand Trunk Express began service in India. Rioting between Muslims and Jews in Jerusalem over access to the Western Wall took place in the Middle East. The centenary of Western Australia was celebrated.

The Kellogg–Briand Pact, a treaty renouncing war as an instrument of national policy, went into effect. In Europe, the Holy See and the Kingdom of Italy signed the Lateran Treaty. The Idionymon law was passed in Greece to outlaw political dissent. Spain hosted the Ibero-American Exposition which featured pavilions from Latin American countries. The German airship LZ 127 *Graf Zeppelin* flew around the world in 21 days.

Contents

Summary

Middle East, Asia, and Pacific Isles

On August 16 of this year the 1929 Palestine riots broke out between Palestinians and Jews over control of the Western Wall. The rioting, initiated in part when British police tore down a screen the Jews had constructed in front of the Wall, continued until the end of the month. In total, 133 Jews and 116 Palestinians were killed. Two of the more famous incidents occurring during these riots were the August 23–24 1929 Hebron massacre, in which almost 70 Jews were killed by Palestinians and the remaining Jews are forced to leave Hebron. The Palestinians had been told that Jews were killing Palestinians. Jews would not return to Hebron until after the Six-Day War in 1967. The other major clash was the 1929 Safed massacre, in which 18–20 Jews were killed by Palestinians in Safed in similar fashion. Elsewhere in the Middle East, Iraq took a big step toward gaining independence from the British. The Iraqi government had, since the end of World War I and the beginning of the British Mandate in the Middle East, consistently resisted British hegemony. In September, Great Britain announced it would support Iraq's inclusion in the League of Nations, signaling the beginning of the end of their direct control of the region.

Early in 1929, the Afghan leader King Amanullah lost power through revolution and civil war to Habibullāh Kalakāni. Habibullāh's rule, however, only lasted nine months. Nadir Shah replaced him in October, starting a line of monarchs which would last 40 years. In India, a general strike in Bombay continued throughout the year despite efforts by the

British. On December 29, the All India Congress in Lahore declared Indian independence from Britain, something it had threatened to do if Britain did not grant India dominion status. China and Russia engaged in a minor conflict after China seized full control of the Manchurian Chinese Eastern Railway. Russia counterattacked and took the cities of Hailar and Manchouli before issuing an ultimatum demanding joint control of the railway to be reinstated. The Chinese agreed to the terms on November 26. The Japanese would later see this defeat as a sign of Chinese weakness, leading to their taking control of Manchuria. The Far East began to experience economic problems late in the year as the effects of the Great Depression began to spread. Southeast Asia was especially hard hit as its exports (spice, rubber, and other commodities) were more sensitive to economic problems. In the Pacific, on December 28 – "Black Saturday" in Samoa – New Zealand colonial police killed 11 unarmed demonstrators, an event which led the Mau movement to demand independence for Samoa.

Europe

Western

In 1929, the Fascist Party in Italy tightened its control. National education policy took a major step towards being completely taken over by the agenda of indoctrination. In that year, the Fascist government took control of the authorization of all textbooks, all secondary school teachers were required to take an oath of loyalty to Fascism, and children began to be taught that they owed the same loyalty to Fascism as they did to God.

On February 11, Mussolini signed the Lateran Treaty, making Vatican City a sovereign state. On July 25, Pope Pius XI emerged from the Vatican and entered St. Peter's Square in a huge procession witnessed by about 250,000 persons, thus ending nearly 60 years of papal self-imprisonment within the Vatican. Italy used the diplomatic prestige associated with this successful agreement to adopt a more aggressive foreign policy. Germany experienced a major turning point in this year due to the economic crash. The country had experienced prosperity under the government of the Weimar Republic until foreign investors withdrew their German interests. This began the crumbling of the Republican government in favor of Nazism. In 1929, the number of unemployed reached three million. On July 27, the Geneva Convention, held in Switzerland, addressed the treatment of prisoners of war in response to problems encountered during World War I.

On May 31, the British general election returned a hung parliament yet again, with the Liberals in position to determine who would have power. These elections were known as the "Flapper" elections due to the fact that it was the first British election in which women under 30 could vote. A week after the vote, on June 7 the Conservatives conceded power rather than ally with the Liberals. Ramsay MacDonald founded a new Labour government the next day.

1929 is regarded as a turning point by French historians, who point out that it was last year in which prosperity was felt before the effects of the Great Depression. The Third Republic had been in power since before World War I. On July 24, French prime minister Raymond Poincaré resigned for medical reasons; he was succeeded by Aristide Briand. Briand adopted a foreign policy of both peace and defensive fortification. The Kellogg–Briand Pact, renouncing war as an instrument of foreign policy, went into effect in this year (it was first signed in Paris in 1928 by most leading world powers). The French began work on the Maginot Line in this year, as a defense against a possible German attack, and on September 5 Briand presented a plan for the *United States of Europe*. On October 22, Briand was replaced as Prime Minister by André Tardieu. Primo de Rivera's dictatorship in Spain experienced growing dissatisfaction among students and academics, as well as businessmen who blamed the government for recent economic woes. Many called for a fascist regime, like that in Italy.

Eastern

In May, Joseph Stalin consolidated his power in the Soviet Union by sending Leon Trotsky into exile. The only country that would grant Trotsky asylum was Turkey, in return for his help during Turkey's civil war. He and his family left the USSR aboard ship on February 12. Stalin turned on his former political ally, Nikolai Bukharin, who was the last real threat to his power. By the end of the year Bukharin had been defeated. Once Stalin was in power, he turned his former support for Lenin's New Economic Policy into opposition. In November, Stalin declared that it "The Year of the Great Breakthrough" and stated that the country would focus on industrial programs as well as on collectivizing the grain supply. He hoped to surpass the West not only in agriculture, but in industry. Millions of Soviet farmers were removed from their private farms, their property was collected, and they were moved to state-owned farms. Stalin emphasized in 1929 a campaign demonizing kulaks as a plague on society. Kulak property was taken and they were deported by cattle train to areas of frozen tundra.

The timber market in Finland began to decline in 1929 due to the Great Depression, as well as the Soviet Union's entrance into the market. Financial and political problems culminated in the birth of the fascist Lapua Movement on November 23 in a demonstration in Lapua. The movement's stated aim was Finnish democracy and anti-communism. The Finnish legislature received heavy pressure to remove basic rights from Communist groups. Politics in Lithuania was heated, as President Voldemaras was unpopular in some quarters, and survived an assassination attempt in Kaunas. Later, while attending a meeting of the League of Nations, he was ousted in a coup by President Smetona, who made himself dictator. Upon Voldemaras' removal from office, Geležinis Vilkas went underground and received aid and encouragement in its activities from Germany. Yugoslavia was renamed the "Kingdom of Yugoslavia" as King Alexander sought to unite the Balkans under his rule. The state's new Monarchy replaced the old parliament, which had been dominated by Serbs.

North America

In October 1929, the British Judicial Committee of the Privy Council overturned a ruling by the Supreme Court of Canada that women could not be members of the legislature. This case, which came to be known as the Persons Case, had important ramifications not just for the rights of women but because in overturning the case, the Judicial Committee of the Privy Council engendered a radical change in the Canadian judicial approach to the Canadian constitution, an approach that has come to be known as the "living tree doctrine". The five women who initiated the case are known in Canada as the Famous Five. In November, the 1929 Grand Banks earthquake occurred off the south coast of Newfoundland in the Atlantic Ocean. It registered as a Richter magnitude 7.2 submarine earthquake centered on Grand Banks, broke 12 submarine transatlantic telegraph cables and triggered a tsunami that destroyed many south coast communities in the Burin Peninsula area, killing 28 (as of 1997, Canada's most lethal earthquake).

The Mexican Cristero War continued in 1929 as clerical forces attempted an assassination of the provisional president in a train bombing in February. The attempt failed. Plutarco Calles, at the center of power for the anti-clerics, continued to gather power in Mexico City. His government was considered an enemy to more conservative Mexicans who held to traditional forms of government and more religious control. Calles founded the National Revolutionary Party early in the year to increase his power; a party which was, ironically, seen by foreigners as fascist and which was in opposition to the Mexican Right. A special election was held in this year, which Jose Vasconselos lost to Ortiz Rubio. By this time, the war had ended. The last group of rebels was defeated on June 4, and in the same month US Ambassador Dwight Morrow initiated talks between parties. On June 21 an agreement was brokered ending the Cristero War. On June 27, church bells rang and mass was held publicly for the first time in three years. The agreement heavily favored the government, as priests were required to register with the government and religion was banned from schools.

The major event of the year for the United States was the stock market crash on Wall Street, which was to have international effects. On September 3, the Dow Jones Industrial Average (DJIA) peaked at 381.17, a height it would not reach again until November 1954. Then, from October 24–October 29, stock prices suffered three multi-digit percentage drops, wiping out more than $30 billion from the New York

Stock Exchange (10 times greater than the annual budget of the federal government). On December 3 U.S. President Herbert Hoover announced to the U.S. Congress that the worst effects of the recent stock market crash were behind the nation, and that the American people had regained faith in the economy.

Literature, arts, and entertainment

Literature of the time reflected the memories many harbored of the horrors of World War I. A major seller was *All Quiet on the Western Front* by Erich Maria Remarque. Remarque was a German who had fought in the war at age eighteen and been wounded in the Third Battle of Ypres. He stated that he intended the book to tell the story "of a generation of men who, even though they may have escaped its shells, were destroyed by the war." Another 1929 book reflecting on World War I was Ernest Hemingway's *A Farewell to Arms*, as well as *Good-Bye to All That* by Robert Graves. In lighter media, a few stars of the comic industry made their debut, including *Tintin*, a comic book character created by Hergé, who would appear in over 200 million comic books in 60 languages. *Popeye*, another comic strip character created by Elzie Crisler Segar, also appeared in this year.

Within the film industry, on May 16 the 1st Academy Awards were presented at the Hollywood Roosevelt Hotel, with *Wings* winning Best Picture. Also, *Hallelujah!* became the first Hollywood film to contain an entirely black cast, and *Atlantic*, a film about the *Titanic*, is an early sound-on-film movie. The arts were in the midst of the Modernist movement, as Pablo Picasso painted two cubist works, *Woman in a Garden* and *Nude in an Armchair*, during this year. The surrealist painters Salvador Dalí and René Magritte completed several works, including *The First Days of Spring* and *The Treachery of Images*. On November 7 in New York City, the Museum of Modern Art opened to the public. The latest in modern architecture was also represented by the Barcelona Pavilion in Spain, and the Royal York Hotel in Toronto, at its completion the tallest building in the British Empire.

Science and technology

The year saw several advances in technology and exploration. On June 27 the first public demonstration of color TV was held by H. E. Ives and his colleagues at Bell Telephone Laboratories in New York. The first images were a bouquet of roses and an American flag. A mechanical system was used to transmit 50-line color television images between New York and Washington. The BBC broadcast a television transmission for the first time. By November, Vladimir Zworykin had taken out the first patent for color television. On November 29, Bernt Balchen, U.S. Admiral Richard Byrd, Captain Ashley McKinley, and Harold June, became the first to fly over the South Pole. Within the year, Britain, Australia and New Zealand began a joint Antarctic Research Expedition, and the German airship *Graf Zeppelin* began a round-the-world flight (ended August 29). This year Ernst Schwarz describes Bonobo (*Pan paniscus*) as a different species from chimpanzee (*Pan troglodites*), both closely related phylogenetically to human beings.

Events

January

- January 1
  - The U.S. Army Air Corps airplane *?* begins a six-day non-stop endurance flight over Southern California using aerial refueling.
  - The British Columbian municipalities of Point Grey and South Vancouver are amalgamated into Vancouver.
- January 6
  - 6 January Dictatorship: King Alexander of the Serbs, Croats, and Slovenes suspends his country's constitution.
  - The Albanian missionary sister Agnes Gonxha Bojaxhiu, later known as Mother Teresa, arrives in Calcutta from Ireland to begin her work in India.
- January 10 – First appearance of Hergé's Belgian comic book hero Tintin as *Tintin in the Land of the Soviets* (*Les Aventures de Tintin,*

reporter..., au pays des Soviets), begins serialization in children's newspaper supplement, *Le Petit Vingtième*.

- January 15 – *Annales d'histoire économique et sociale* begins publication in France.
- January 17 – First appearance of comic strip hero Popeye in *Thimble Theatre*.
- January 29 – *All Quiet on the Western Front* (*Im Westen nichts Neues*), by Erich Maria Remarque, is published in book form.

February

-
- February 9 – "Litvinov's Pact" is signed in Moscow by the Soviet Union, Poland, Estonia, Romania and Latvia who agree not to use force to settle disputes between themselves.
- February 11 – The Kingdom of Italy and the Holy See of the Catholic Church sign the Lateran Treaty to establish the Vatican City as an independent sovereign enclave within Rome, resolving the "Roman Question".
- February 14 – "Saint Valentine's Day Massacre": Five gangsters (rivals of Al Capone), plus two civilians, are shot dead in Chicago.
- February 26 – The Grand Teton National Park is established by the United States Congress.

February 26: Grand Teton National Park.

March

- March 2 – The longest bridge in the world at this time, the San Francisco Bay Toll-Bridge, opens.

- March 3 – A revolt by Generals José Gonzalo Escobar and Jesús María Aguirre fails in Mexico.
- March 4
  - Herbert Hoover is inaugurated as the 31st President of the United States, succeeding Calvin Coolidge.
  - Establishment of the National Revolutionary Party (*Partido Nacional Revolucionario*) in Mexico by ex-President Plutarco Elías Calles. Under a succession of names, it will hold power in the country continuously for the next 71 years.
- March 28 – Japanese forces withdraw from Shandong province to their garrison in Tsingtao bringing an end to the Jinan Incident.
- March 30 – Imperial Airways begins operating the first commercial flights between London and Karachi.

April

-
- April 3 – Persia signs the Litvinov Protocol.
- April 4 – Karl Benz the creator of the first automobile dies.
- April 14 – The inaugural Monaco Grand Prix is won by William Grover-Williams driving a Bugatti.

May

- May – The Wickersham Commission begins its investigation of organized crime following alcohol Prohibition in the United States.
- May 1 – The 7.2 Mw Kopet Dag earthquake shakes the Iran-Turkmenistan border region with a maximum Mercalli intensity of IX (*Violent*), killing up to 3,800 and injuring 1,121.
- May 7 – "The Battle Of Blood Alley" is fought by a razor gang in Sydney, Australia
- May 16 – The 1st Academy Awards are presented in a 15-minute ceremony at the Hollywood Roosevelt Hotel, honoring the best movies of 1927 and 1928, *Wings* (1927) winning Best Picture. Gerald Duffy (died 1928) receives the only Academy Award for Best Title Writing ever awarded (for his intertitles to the silent film *The Private Life of Helen of Troy* (1927)).

- May 31 – The United Kingdom general election again returns a hung parliament; the Liberals in Parliament determine which party will govern.

June

- June 1 – The 1st Conference of the Communist Parties of Latin America is held in Buenos Aires.
- June 3 – The Treaty of Lima settles a border dispute between Peru and Chile.
- June 7 – The Lateran Treaty, making Vatican City a sovereign state, is ratified.
- June 8 – Ramsay MacDonald forms the United Kingdom's second Labour government.
- June 21 – An agreement brokered by U.S. Ambassador Dwight Whitney Morrow helps end the Cristero War in Mexico.
- June 27 – The first public demonstration of color TV is held, by H. E. Ives and his colleagues at Bell Telephone Laboratories in New York. The first images are a bouquet of roses and an American flag. A mechanical system is used to transmit 50-line color television images between New York and Washington.

July

- July 11 – In Russia, a secret decree of the Sovnarkom creates the backbone of the Gulag system.
- July 24
  - French prime minister Raymond Poincaré resigns and is succeeded by Aristide Briand.
  - The Kellogg–Briand Pact, renouncing war as an instrument of foreign policy, goes into effect (it was first signed in Paris on August 27, 1928 by most leading world powers).
- July 25 – Pope Pius XI emerges from the Apostolic Palace and enters St. Peter's Square in a huge procession witnessed by about 250,000 persons, thus ending nearly 60 years of self-imposed status by the papacy as Prisoner in the Vatican.
- July 27

- o The Geneva Convention addresses the treatment of prisoners of war.
- o Red Crescent adopted as an additional emblem of the League of Red Cross Societies.

August

- August 8–29 – German rigid airship LZ 127 *Graf Zeppelin* makes a circumnavigation of the Northern Hemisphere eastabout out of Lakehurst, New Jersey, including the first nonstop flight of any kind across the Pacific Ocean (Tokyo–Los Angeles).
- August 16 – The 1929 Palestine riots break out between Palestinians and Jews in Mandatory Palestine and continue until the end of the month. In total, 133 Jews and 116 Palestinians are killed.
- August 20 – First transmissions of John Logie Baird's experimental 30-line television system by the British Broadcasting Corporation.
- August 23–24 – The 1929 Hebron massacre, in which 65–68 Jews are killed by Palestinians and the remaining Jews are forced to leave Hebron.
- August 29
  - o The 1929 Safed massacre, in which 18–20 Jews are killed in Safed by Palestinian Arabs.
  - o The SS *San Juan* collides with the oil tanker *S.C.T. Dodd* off the California coast, causing the *San Juan* to sink in 3 minutes, killing 77 people.
- August 31 – The Young Plan, which sets the total World War I reparations owed by Germany at US$26,350,000,000 to be paid over a period of 58½ years, is finalized.

September

- September 3 – The Dow Jones Industrial Average peaks at 381.17, a height it will not reach again until November 1954.
- September 5 – Aristide Briand presents his plan for the *United States of Europe*.

- September 17 – A coup ousts Augustinas Voldemaras in Lithuania; the new president is Antanas Smetona.
- September 30 – Fritz von Opel pilots the first rocket-powered aircraft, the Opel RAK.1, in front of a large crowd in Frankfurt am Main.

October

- October 14 – The Philadelphia Athletics win the World Series four games to one over the Chicago Cubs, taking Game Five by a 3-2 score at Shibe Park.
- October 18 – On appeal from the Supreme Court of Canada on behalf of "The Famous Five" Canadian women in the landmark case of *Edwards v. Canada (Attorney General)*, the Judicial Committee of the Privy Council in the United Kingdom announces that women are "persons" under the British North America Acts and thus eligible for appointment to the Senate of Canada.
- October 22 – The government of Aristide Briand falls in France.

The Wall Street Crash of 1929, the beginning of the Great Depression

- October 24–29 – Wall Street Crash of 1929: Three multi-digit percentage drops wipe out more than $30 billion from the New

York Stock Exchange (10 times greater than the annual budget of the federal government).
- October 25 – Former U.S. Interior Secretary Albert B. Fall is convicted of bribery for his role in the Teapot Dome scandal, becoming the first Presidential cabinet member to go to prison for actions in office.

November

- November – Vladimir Zworykin takes out the first patent for color television.
- November 1
  - An annular solar eclipse is seen over the Atlantic Ocean and Africa.
  - Conscription in Australia ends.
- November 7 – In New York City, the Museum of Modern Art (MoMA) opens to the public. The first exhibition 'Cézanne, Gauguin, van Gogh and Seurat' (Nov 7 - Dec 7) was seen by 47.000 visitors, curator is Alfred H. Barr.
- November 15 – U.K. release of *Atlantic*, a film about the sinking of the RMS *Titanic* which is one of the first British sound-on-film movies and, in its simultaneously-shot German-language version, the first to be released in Germany.
- November 18 – 1929 Grand Banks earthquake.
- November 29 – Bernt Balchen, U.S. Admiral Richard Byrd, Captain Ashley McKinley and Harold June become the first to fly over the South Pole.

December

- December 28 – "Black Saturday" in Samoa: New Zealand colonial police kill 11 unarmed demonstrators, an event which leads the Mau movement to demand independence for Samoa.
- December 29 – The All India Congress in Lahore demands Indian independence.

Births

January

Sergio Leone

Martin Luther King Jr.

Rudolf Mössbauer

- January 1
  - Raymond Chow, Hong Kong film producer
  - Joseph Lombardo, American mafioso
  - Haruo Nakajima, Japanese actor
- January 3
  - Sergio Leone, Italian director (d. 1989)
  - Ernst Mahle, Brazilian composer

- o Gordon Moore, American computing entrepreneur and benefactor
- January 4 – Günter Schabowski, official of the Socialist Unity Party of Germany (d. 2015)
- January 5 – Wilbert Harrison, American singer (d. 1994)
- January 7 – Terry Moore, American actress
- January 8
  - o Saeed Jaffrey, Indian-born actor (d. 2015)
  - o Erich Jantsch, Austrian astrophysicist (d. 1980)
- January 9 – Brian Friel, Irish dramatist (d. 2015)
- January 12
  - o Alasdair MacIntyre, Scottish-born American philosopher
  - o Jaakko Hintikka, Finnish philosopher and logician (d. 2015)
- January 15 – Martin Luther King Jr., American civil rights leader, Nobel laureate (d. 1968)
- January 17
  - o Elaine Roth, American female professional baseball player (d. 2007)
  - o Tan Boon Teik, Attorney-General of Singapore (d. 2012)
- January 20 – Arte Johnson, American actor
- January 23 – John Charles Polanyi, Canadian chemist, Nobel laureate
- January 25 – Benny Golson, American jazz musician
- January 28 -- Claes Oldenburg, American artist Clothespin (Oldenburg)
- January 29 – George Ross Anderson, Jr., United States federal judge
- January 27 – Mohamed Al-Fayed, Egyptian business magnate
- January 31
  - o Rudolf Mössbauer, German physicist, Nobel laureate (d. 2011)
  - o Jean Simmons, English-American actress (d. 2010)

February

Pierre Brice

James Hong

- February 2
    - Věra Chytilová, Czech director (d. 2014)
    - John Henry Holland, American computer scientist (d. 2015)
- February 3 – Huntington Hardisty, American admiral (d. 2003)
- February 4 – Jerry Adler, American actor
- February 5 – Luc Ferrari, French composer (d. 2005)
- February 6
    - Colin Murdoch, New Zealand pharmacist, veterinarian and inventor (d. 2008)
    - Sixten Jernberg, Swedish cross-country skier (d. 2012)
    - Pierre Brice, French actor (d. 2015)
- February 10
    - Hallgeir Brenden, Norwegian cross-country skier (d. 2007)
    - Jerry Goldsmith, American composer and conductor (d. 2004)
- February 14 – Vic Morrow, American actor and director (d. 1982)
- February 15
    - Graham Hill, English race car driver (d. 1975)
    - Kauko Armas Nieminen, Finnish physicist

- o James Schlesinger, American politician (d. 2014)
- February 17 – Patricia Routledge, English actress and singer
- February 18 – Len Deighton, British author
- February 22 – James Hong, Chinese American actor and director
- February 24 – Zdzisław Beksiński, Polish surrealist painter (d. 2005)

March

Lennart Meri

- March 1 – Georgi Markov, Bulgarian dissident (d. 1978)
- March 8 – Hebe Camargo, Brazilian television presenter, actress and singer (d. 2012)
- March 8 -- Nicodemo Scarfo, American mafioso
- March 9 – Zillur Rahman, Bangladeshi politician (also President (d. 2013)
- March 13 – Peter Breck, American actor and drama teacher (d. 2012)
- March 18 – Christa Wolf, German literary critic, novelist, and essayist (d. 2011)
- March 19 – Miquel Martí i Pol, Catalan poet (d. 2003)
- March 20
    - o William Andrew MacKay, Canadian lawyer and judge (d. 2013)
    - o Herbert Wilson, Welsh physicist and biophysicist (d. 2008)
- March 23 – Sir Roger Bannister, British athlete
- March 25 – Cecil Taylor, American free jazz pianist and composer

- March 27 – Rita Briggs, American female professional baseball player (d. 1994)
- March 29 – Lennart Meri, President of Estonia (d. 2006)

April

Max von Sydow

- April 1
  - Barbara Bryne, British actress
  - Milan Kundera, Czech writer
  - Jane Powell, American actress and dancer
- April 2 – Ed Dorn, American poet (d. 1999)
- April 3 – Poul Schlüter, Danish politician
- April 5 – Ivar Giaever, Norwegian physicist, Nobel Prize laureate
- April 10 – Max von Sydow, Swedish actor
- April 14
  - Paavo Berglund, Finnish conductor and violinist (d. 2012)
  - Gerry Anderson, English television and film producer, director, writer (*Thunderbirds*) (d. 2012)
- April 14 – Chadli Bendjedid, President of Algeria (d. 2012)
- April 17 – James Last, German composer (d. 2015)
- April 22 – Michael Atiyah, British-Lebanese mathematician
- April 26 – Alexandre Lamfalussy, Hungarian-born Belgian economist and central banker (d. 2015)
- April 30 – Klausjürgen Wussow, German theatre- and television actor (d. 2007)

May

Audrey Hepburn

Peter Higgs

- May 1 – Ralf Dahrendorf, Anglo-German sociologist (d. 2009)
- May 2
  - Link Wray, American rock and roll musician (d. 2005)
  - Édouard Balladur, Prime Minister of France
- May 3
  - Denise Lor, American popular music singer and actress (d. 2015)
  - Per-Ingvar Brånemark, Swedish physician and "father of modern dental implantology" (d. 2014)
- May 4
  - Ronald Golias, Brazilian comedian and actor (d. 2005)
  - Audrey Hepburn, British actress and activist (d. 1993)
- May 5 – Ilene Woods, American singer and actress (d. 2010)
- May 6 – Paul Lauterbur, American chemist, Nobel laureate (d. 2007)
- May 8
  - Miyoshi Umeki, Japanese singer and actress (d. 2007)
  - Jane Roberts, American writer (d. 1984)

- May 10 – Betty Foss, American female professional baseball player (d. 1998)
- May 11 – Margaret Kerry, American actress
- May 12 – Sam Nujoma, first President of Namibia
- May 16 – Adrienne Rich, American poet and essayist (d. 2012)
- May 20 – Ahmed Hamdi, Egyptian soldier (d. 1973)
- May 25 – Beverly Sills, American operatic soprano; later director of the New York City Opera (d. 2007)
- May 26 – Lloyd Reckord, Jamaican actor, filmmaker and director (d. 2015)
- May 29 – Peter Higgs, British theoretical physicist, Nobel Prize laureate

June

Karolos Papoulias

- June 3
  - Werner Arber, Swiss microbiologist, Nobel laureate
  - Chuck Barris, American television game show host and producer
- June 4 – Karolos Papoulias, President of Greece
- June 6 – Sunil Dutt, Hindi film actor (d. 2005)
- June 7 – John Turner, 17th Prime Minister of Canada
- June 10
  - Harald Juhnke, German actor and comedian (d. 2005)
  - E. O. Wilson, American biologist

- June 11 – Dolores Ashcroft-Nowicki, British occult writer#
- June 12 – Anne Frank, German-born diarist and Holocaust victim (d. 1945)
- June 16 – Paul Cain, American Pentecostal Christian evangelist
- June 18 – Jürgen Habermas, German sociologist and philosopher
- June 20
  - Anne Weale, British writer (d. 2007)
  - Larry Collins, American novelist (d. 2005)
- June 25 – Eric Carle, American designer, illustrator, and writer
- June 26 – Milton Glaser, American graphic designer, illustrator and teacher
- June 29 – Oriana Fallaci, Italian journalist and author (d. 2006)

July

Imelda Marcos

Hassan II of Morocco

Jacqueline Kennedy Onassis

- July 1 – Gerald Edelman, American biologist, Nobel laureate (d. 2014)
- July 2 – Imelda Marcos, First Lady of the Philippines
- July 5
  - Chikao Ōtsuka, Japanese actor and voice actor, father of Akio Ōtsuka (d. 2015)
  - Katherine Helmond, American actress
  - Thérèse Quentin, French actress (d. 2015)
- July 9 – King Hassan II of Morocco (d. 1999)
- July 11 – David Kelly, Irish actor (d. 2012)
- July 19 – Alice Pollitt, American female professional baseball player (d. 2016)
- Gaston Glock, Austrian Inventor and Businessman
- July 22 – U. A. Fanthorpe, British poet (d. 2009)
- July 25 – Vasily Shukshin, Russian actor, writer, screenwriter and film director (d. 1974)
- July 27
  - Jean Baudrillard, French sociologist, philosopher, cultural theorist and political commentator (d. 2007)
  - Jack Higgins, British novelist
- July 28 – Jacqueline Kennedy Onassis, American First Lady (d. 1994)
- July 31 – Don Murray, American actor

August

Yasser Arafat

- August 1
  - Samuel Charters, American writer, music historian and record producer (d. 2015)
  - Hafizullah Amin, Afghan politician and statesman (d. 1979)
- August 5 – Ottó Boros, Hungarian water polo player (d. 1988)
- August 8 – Ronnie Biggs, British criminal (d. 2013)
- August 17 – Francis Gary Powers, American U-2 spy plane pilot (d. 1977)
- August 23 – Zoltán Czibor, Hungarian footballer (d. 1997)
- August 24 – Yasser Arafat, Palestinian leader, Nobel laureate (d. 2004)
- August 27 – Ralph T. Coe, American art historian of Native American art (d. 2010)
- August 29 – Lorenz Weinrich, German historian

September

- September 1 – "Mad Dog" Vachon, Canadian professional wrestler (d. 2013)
- September 3 – Whitey Bulger, incarcerated American organized crime boss
- September 4 – Thomas Eagleton, United States Senator for Missouri (1969–87) (d. 2007)
- September 5 – Bob Newhart, American comedian and actor
- September 10 – Arnold Palmer, American golfer
- September 14 – Hans Clarin, German actor (d. 2005)

- September 15 – Murray Gell-Mann, American physicist, Nobel laureate
- September 16 – Maxine Kline, American female professional baseball player
- September 19 – Mel Stewart, African-American actor (d. 2002)
- September 20 – Anne Meara, American actress and comedian (d. 2015)
- September 21 – Sándor Kocsis, Hungarian football player (d. 1979)
- September 22 – Hédi Váradi, Hungarian actress (d. 1987)
- September 25
  - Barbara Walters, American journalist
  - Ronnie Barker, English actor, comedian and writer (d. 2005)
- September 28 – Lata Mangeshkar, Indian singer

October

Ursula K. Le Guin

- October 2 – Moses Gunn, African-American actor (d. 1993)
- October 7 – Tony Beckley, English character actor (d. 1980)
- October 11 – Liselotte Pulver, Swiss actress
- October 13 – Walasse Ting, Chinese-American painter (d. 2010)
- October 15 – Antonino Zichichi, Italian physicist
- October 18 – Violeta Chamorro, President of Nicaragua
- October 20 – Colin Jeavons, Welsh actor
- October 21 – Ursula K. Le Guin, American science-fiction and fantasy author
- October 22 – Lev Yashin, Russian footballer (d. 1990)
- October 24 – Clifford Rose, British classical actor

- October 29 – Yevgeny Primakov, Russian politician and diplomat (d. 2015)

November

Imre Kertész

Grace Kelly

- November 2
  - Rachel Ames, American actress
  - Richard E. Taylor, Canadian-born physicist, Nobel laureate
- November 6 – June Squibb, American actress
- November 7
  - Eric R. Kandel, Austrian-born neuroscientist, Nobel laureate
  - Lila Kaye, British actress (d. 2012)
- November 9 – Imre Kertész, Hungarian writer, Nobel laureate (d. 2016)
- November 12
  - Grace Kelly, American actress; later Princess of Monaco (d. 1982)
  - Michael Ende, German writer of fantasy (d. 1995)
- November 13 – Fred Phelps, American pastor, activist (Westboro Baptist Church) (d. 2014)
- November 15 – Edward Asner, American actor
- November 17 – Gorō Naya, Japanese actor, voice actor, narrator and theatre director, older brother of Rokurō Naya (d. 2013)
- November 18 – John McMartin, American actor

- November 23 – Hal Lindsey, American Christian evangelist
- November 24 – Franciszek Kokot, Polish nephrologist
- November 28 – Berry Gordy, American record producer and songwriter
- November 30 – Dick Clark, American television entertainer (d. 2012)

December

Christopher Plummer

- December 6 – Nikolaus Harnoncourt, Austrian conductor (d. 2016)
- December 9 – Bob Hawke, 23rd Prime Minister of Australia
- December 13 – Christopher Plummer, Canadian actor
- December 16 – Nicholas Courtney, British actor (d. 2011)
- December 17 – William Safire, American author, columnist, journalist, and presidential speechwriter (d. 2009)
- December 23 – Chet Baker, American jazz musician (d. 1988)
- December 29
  - Susie Garrett, American actress (d. 2002)
  - Peter May, English cricketer (d. 1994)
- December 31 – Mies Bouwman, Dutch television presenter

Deaths

January

Ferdinand Foch

Karl Benz

- January 5
  - Marc McDermott, Australian-American actor (b. 1881)
  - Grand Duke Nicholas Nikolaevich of Russia (b. 1856)
- January 13 – Wyatt Earp, American gunfighter (b. 1848)
- January 15 – George Cope, American painter (b. 1855)
  - William Boyd Dawkins, British geologist and archaeologist (b. 1837)
- January 24 – Wilfred Baddeley, English tennis player (b. 1872)
- January 30
  - Franklin J. Drake, American admiral (b. 1846)
  - La Goulue, French dancer (b. 1866)

February

- February 3 – José Gutiérrez Guerra, 28th President of Bolivia (b. 1869)

- February 6 – Maria Christina of Austria, Queen Regent of Spain (b. 1858)
- February 11 – Johann II, Prince of Liechtenstein (b. 1840)
- February 12 – Lillie Langtry, British singer and actress (b. 1853)
- February 14 – Thomas Burke, American sprinter (b. 1875)
- February 18 – William Russell, American actor (b. 1884)
- February 24 – Frank Keenan, American actor (b. 1858)
- February 27 – Briton Hadden, co-founder of *Time* magazine (b. 1898)

March

- March 1 – Royal H. Weller, American politician (b. 1881)
- March 2 – Sir Edward Hobart Seymour, British admiral (b. 1840)
- March 5 – David Dunbar Buick, Scottish-American inventor (b. 1854)
- March 12 – Asa Griggs Candler, American businessman and politician (b. 1851)
- March 15 – Pinetop Smith, American blues pianist (b. 1904)
- March 18 – William P. Cronan, Naval Governor of Guam (b. 1879)
- March 20 – Ferdinand Foch, French commander of Allied forces in World War I (b. 1851)

April

- April 4
  - Karl Benz, German automotive pioneer (b. 1844)
  - William Michael Crose, United States Navy Commander and the seventh Naval Governor of American Samoa (b. 1867)
- April 12 – Enrico Ferri, Italian criminologist (b. 1856)
- April 22 – Henry Lerolle, French painter (b. 1848)
- April 24 – Caroline Rémy de Guebhard, French feminist (b. 1855)

May

- May 2
  - Charalambos Tseroulis, Greek general (b. 1879)

- ○ Segundo de Chomón, Spanish film director (b. 1871)
- May 21 – Archibald Primrose, former Prime Minister of the United Kingdom (b. 1847)

June

- June 8 – Bliss Carman, Canadian poet (b. 1861)
- June 11 – William Dickson Boyce, American entrepreneur and founder of the Boy Scouts of America (b. 1858)
- June 16 – Bramwell Booth, General of The Salvation Army (b. 1856)
- June 26 – Amandus Adamson, Estonian sculptor (b. 1855)
- June 28 – Edward Carpenter, English poet (b. 1844)

July

Georges Clemenceau

Emile Berliner

Wilhelm Maybach

- July 2 – Gladys Brockwell, American actress (b. 1893)
- July 3 – Dustin Farnum, American actor (b. 1874)
- July 12 – Robert Henri, American painter (b. 1865)
- July 15 – Hugo von Hofmannsthal, Austrian writer (b. 1874)
- July 28 – Hertha Hanfstaengl, second child and only daughter of Ernst Hanfstaengl (b. 1924)
- August – Mary MacLane, Canadian feminist writer (b. 1881)

August

- August 3
  - Emile Berliner, German-born inventor (b. 1851)
  - Thorstein Veblen, Norwegian-American economist (b. 1857)
- August 5 – Dame Millicent Fawcett, British suffragist and feminist (b. 1847)
- August 14 – Henry Horne, 1st Baron Horne, British general (b. 1861)
- August 19 – Sergei Diaghilev, Russian ballet impresario (b. 1872)
- August 22 – Otto Liman von Sanders, German general (b. 1855)
- August 26 – Sir Ernest Satow, British diplomat and scholar (b. 1843)
- August 27 – Herman Potočnik Noordung, Slovenian rocket engineer (b. 1892)

September

- September 2 – Paul Leni, German filmmaker (b. 1885)
- September 12 – Rainis, Latvian poet and playwright (b. 1865)
- September 23 – Richard Adolf Zsigmondy, Austrian-born chemist, Nobel Prize laureate (b. 1865)
- September 24 – Mahidol Adulyadej, Thai doctor and father of King Rama IX (b. 1892)
- September 25 – Miller Huggins, American baseball manager and MLB Hall of Famer (b. 1879)
- September 26 – Aby Warburg, German historian and cultural theorist (b. 1866)

- September 27 – Johnny Hill. British, European, and World flyweight boxing champion (b. 1905)
- September 29 – Tanaka Giichi, 26th Prime Minister of Japan (b. 1864)

October

Gustav Stresemann

Bernhard von Bülow

- October 1 – Antoine Bourdelle, French sculptor (b. 1861)
- October 3
  - Jeanne Eagels, American actress (b. 1890)
  - Gustav Stresemann, Chancellor of Germany, recipient of the Nobel Peace Prize (b. 1878)
- October 27 – Georg von der Marwitz, German general (b. 1856)
- October 28 – Bernhard von Bülow, Chancellor of Germany (b. 1849)
- October 29 – Emily Robin, English Madame (b. 1874)

November

- November 1 – Habibullāh Kalakāni, deposed Emir of Afghanistan (b. 1891)
- November 6 – Prince Maximilian of Baden, Chancellor of Germany (b. 1867)
- November 14 – Joe McGinnity, American baseball player and MLB Hall of Famer (b. 1871)
- November 15 – Léon Delacroix, former Prime Minister of Belgium (b. 1867)
- November 17 – Herman Hollerith, American businessman and inventor (b. 1860)
- November 24
    - Georges Clemenceau, Premier of France (b. 1841)
    - Raymond Hitchcock, American actor (b. 1865)

December

Wilhelm Maybach

- December 10
    - Frederick Abberline, Chief Inspector of the London Metropolitan Police and investigator in the Jack the Ripper murders (b. 1843)
    - Harry Crosby, American publisher and poet (b. 1898)
- December 14 – Henry B. Jackson, British admiral (b. 1855)
- December 17
    - Manuel de Oliveira Gomes da Costa, Portuguese general and politician, tenth President of the Portuguese Republic (b. 1863)
    - Arthur G. Jones-Williams, British aviator (b. 1898)

- December 20 – Émile Loubet, French politician, 8th President of France (b. 1838)
- December 21 – I. L. Patterson, American politician, 18th Governor of Oregon (b. 1859)
- December 26 – Albert Giraud, Belgian poet (b. 1860)
- December 29 – Wilhelm Maybach, German automobile designer (b. 1846)

Date unknown

- Emma Curtis Hopkins, American writer (b. 1849)

Nobel Prizes

- Physics – Louis de Broglie
- Chemistry – Arthur Harden, Hans Karl August Simon von Euler-Chelpin
- Physiology or Medicine – Christiaan Eijkman, Sir Frederick Gowland Hopkins
- Literature – Thomas Mann
- Peace – Frank Billings Kellogg

In the News

The Wall Street Crash of 1929.

The St. Valentine's Day Massacre on February 14th. Seven gangsters rivaling Al Capone are murdered in Chicago, Illinois.

Popeye, a comic strip character created by Elzie Crisler Segar, makes his debut.

The United States and Canada sign an agreement to protect Niagara Falls.

Academy Awards, popularly known as the Oscars, are started.

The First Public phone booths appear in London.

The German airship Graf Zeppelin completes a round-the-world flight.

British General Election 1929 Ramsay MacDonald (Labor) defeats Stanley Baldwin (Conservative)